Rodent rap

Bobbie Kalman

🌱 Crabtree Publishing Company

www.crabtreebooks.com

Created by Bobbie Kalman

Author and Editor-in-Chief
Bobbie Kalman

Educational consultants
Reagan Miller
Joan King
Elaine Hurst

Editors
Reagan Miller
Joan King
Kathy Middleton

Proofreader
Crystal Sikkens

Photo research
Bobbie Kalman

Design
Bobbie Kalman
Katherine Berti

Production coordinator
Katherine Berti

Prepress technician
Katherine Berti

Photographs and illustrations
Barbara Bedell: p. 3 (illustration)
BigStockPhoto: p. 10 (bottom)
iStockphoto: p. 11 (top left)
Shutterstock: cover, p. 1, 3, 4, 5, 6, 7, 8,
    10 (top), 11 (bottom), 12, 13, 14, 15, 16

Library and Archives Canada Cataloguing in Publication

Kalman, Bobbie, 1947-
    Rodent rap / Bobbie Kalman.

(My world)
ISBN 978-0-7787-9438-7 (bound).--ISBN 978-0-7787-9482-0 (pbk.)

1. Rodents--Juvenile literature. I. Title.
II. Series: My world (St. Catharines, Ont.).

QL737.R6K335 2010   j599.35   C2009-906097-3

Library of Congress Cataloging-in-Publication Data

Kalman, Bobbie.
 Rodent rap / Bobbie Kalman.
    p. cm. -- (My world)
 ISBN 978-0-7787-9482-0 (pbk. : alk. paper) -- ISBN 978-0-7787-9438-7
(reinforced library binding : alk. paper)
 1. Rodents--Juvenile literature. I. Title. II. Series.

 QL737.R6K2845 2010
 599.35--dc22

                                                                    2009041213

Crabtree Publishing Company

www.crabtreebooks.com   1-800-387-7650

Printed in China/122009/CT20091009

Published in Canada
Crabtree Publishing
616 Welland Ave.
St. Catharines, Ontario
L2M 5V6

Published in the United States
Crabtree Publishing
PMB 59051
350 Fifth Avenue, 59th Floor
New York, New York 10118

Published in the United Kingdom
Crabtree Publishing
Maritime House
Basin Road North, Hove
BN41 1WR

Published in Australia
Crabtree Publishing
386 Mt. Alexander Rd.
Ascot Vale (Melbourne)
VIC 3032

Words to know

beaver

chipmunk

quills

porcupine

rat

rodent teeth

3

Some **rodents** are small, and some are big.
One is called a hog, and one is called a pig,
but a rodent is not a pig or a hog,
and a prairie dog is not really a dog!
These animals are rodents. Take a look!
Then read the rodent rap in this book.

groundhog

guinea pig

prairie dog

The smallest rodent is the jerboa.

The biggest is the capybara.

Do you have hamsters living in your house, or is your pet rodent a cute little mouse?

mouse

hamsters

Rodents are animals with four sharp teeth!
Two are on top and two are underneath.
These four teeth never stop growing.
They are the teeth that this groundhog
is showing.

groundhog

"To keep our teeth short, we chew and chew. Chewing is something we have to do. We chew on nutshells, we chew on wood. Wood does not taste very good!"

beaver

"We are rodents with very sharp **spines**.
We are prickly porcupines.
Our spines, called **quills**,
come out of our skin.
If you come too close,
you would wish
they stayed in."

quills

6

porcupines

"I am a rodent called a rat.
My best friend is a cat.
A cat is not a rodent,
but we like each other.
To me, this cat is like a brother!"

rat   cat

"Sometimes he lets me
sit on his head.
I sleep on his fur.
It makes a soft bed."

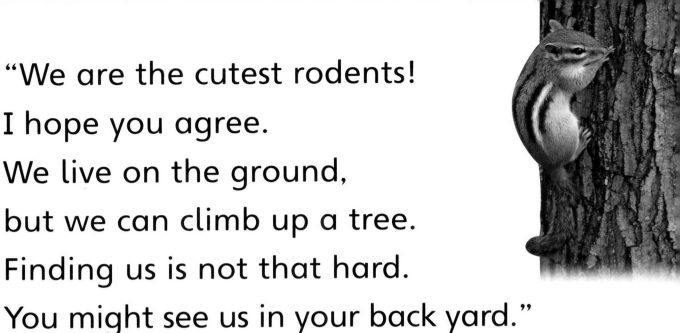

"We are the cutest rodents!
I hope you agree.
We live on the ground,
but we can climb up a tree.
Finding us is not that hard.
You might see us in your back yard."

"We are
chipmunks!"

"We can fit in a glove,
we are so small."

"When we stand on a
mountain, we look tall."

"We stand on our back legs.
Sometimes we dance!"

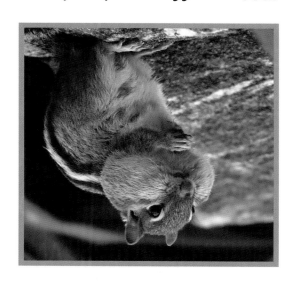

"We stuff our cheeks
when we have a chance."

"We are rodents called prairie dogs.
Our home is an underground **town**.
We come up each day
to find some food,
and then we go back down."

"We guard our town and look all around."

"Often, we huddle and have a group cuddle."

Notes for adults

What is rap?
Rap is part speech, poetry, and song. Rapping is part of hip-hop music. It can be spoken over a beat or on its own. Most children love it! *Rodent rap* is a fun way to learn about a group of animals called rodents. This book not only teaches children about these animals, but it is an excellent opportunity to get them rapping about all kinds of subjects. It is a fun motivational tool!

Rapping about this and that
Groups of children could pick animals or other topics and make up rap songs about them. They can then perform their songs for the class. Rhyming is an excellent way to teach words that sound the same, and rapping is a great way to practice keeping the beat. Exact rhyme is not necessary, nor is rhyme itself even necessary, as long as there is a distinct beat.

Their stories in rap
Groups of children could make up rap stories and perform them with musical instruments such as drums and shakers. They could read "Hip-hop dancers" and also make up dances to go with their rap songs about their families, friends, or life at school. A rap starter might be "School is really cool!"